Flavors of Pakistan

Discover the Flavors of Pakistan with These Delicious Recipes!

BY: Allie Allen

Copyright Notes

Table of Contents

Introduction

If you're looking to jazz up your daily meals with a little boost of flavor, then this Pakistani recipe book is exactly what you need! Filled with 30 delicious recipes that are aromatic and chockful of flavor, this recipe book is filled to the brim with deliciousness and with its help, you'll be able to put up all sorts of amazing dishes!

From Kebabs to Ladoos, this book has it all! Plus, all of the recipes are simple, easy-to-follow and come with step-by-step directions, making sure you put up amazing dishes every time!

So what are you waiting for? Choose a recipe and let's get started!

Lahori Fish Fry

A popular street food favorite from Lahore - Spicy fish pieces are coated in a crispy exterior for an absolutely delicious appetizer.

Makes: 6 servings

Prep: 25 mins

Cook: 10 mins

Ingredients:

Marinade

- 2 lb. fish fillet of your choice, cut into pieces
- 2 tbsp. garlic paste
- 2 tsp. salt
- ½ cup lemon juice

Coating

- 2 tbsp. cumin seeds
- 5 tbsp. cilantro seeds
- 5 tbsp. chickpea flour
- 1 tbsp. chili flakes
- 1 tbsp. fenugreek
- 1 tbsp. turmeric
- Water
- ½ cup oil for frying
- 3 tbsp. chaat masala

Directions:

In a bowl, mix together the marinating and all the fish to marinate for at least 20 minutes.

In a mixer or in a mortar and pestle, roughly grind the cumin and cilantro seeds.

In a separate bowl, sieve in the chickpea flour. Add the chili flakes, ground cumin and cilantro seeds, fenugreek, and turmeric. Mix thoroughly.

Add in a little water to this mixture to make a very thick paste. Add this paste to the fix and combine evenly.

Heat oil and fry fish on all sides until golden brown. This should not take more than 4 minutes.

Drain on a paper towel to absorb excess oil.

Sprinkle with chaat masala immediately and serve! The fish works best with mint chutney.

Chicken Kadai

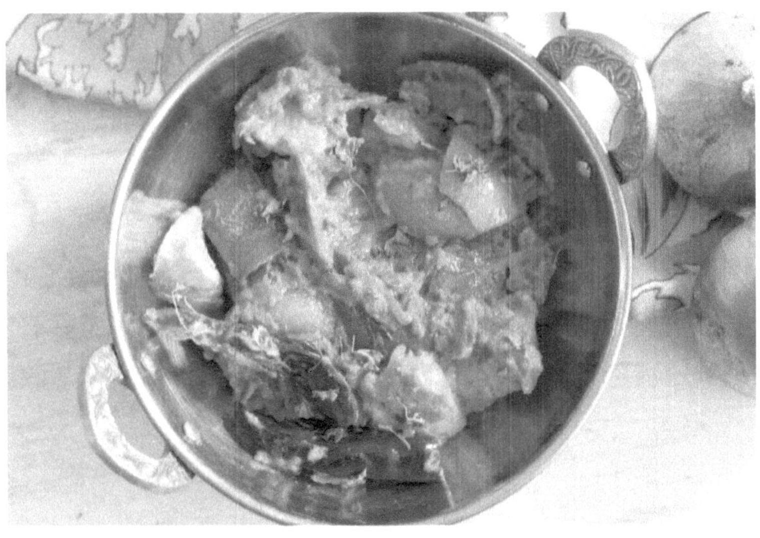

Combine together powerful flavors and aromatics and you'd get Chicken Kadai! Succulent chicken is cooked in a rich tomato based gravy that is widely popular in Pakistan!

Makes: 6 servings

Prep: 35 mins

Cook: 30 mins

Ingredients:

Marinate

- 1 whole chicken, skin removed, cut into 12 pieces.
- ½ tbsp. ginger paste
- 1 tsp. red chili powder
- 1 tbsp. garlic paste
- 1 tsp cumin powder
- ¼ tsp turmeric powder
- 1 tsp cilantro powder
- Red food coloring (optional)
- 1 tsp salt
- 1 tbsp. lemon juice

Other

- 10-12 curry leaves
- 1 tbsp. garlic, crushed
- 1 inch piece of ginger, finely chopped
- 2 green chilies, chopped
- 1 medium onion, finely chopped
- 4 medium tomatoes, chopped
- ½ cup fresh cilantro leaves, divided
- ½ cup water

- 4 tbsp. oil

Directions:

Wash and dry the chicken pieces.

Mix all the marinate Ingredients together and add the chicken. Leave to marinate for at least 30 minutes.

Once marinated, heat 4 tbsp. of oil. Add in the curry leaves, ginger, and garlic. Cook for 20 seconds and then add in the chilies and onion. Cook until the onion turns translucent – about 2 minutes.

Next add in the chopped tomatoes. Cook until the tomatoes are soft.

Add in the chicken. Season with salt according to taste.

Cook on high, stirring occasionally until oil rises to the top. This should take about 5 minutes.

After the oil appears, lower the heat and add in the water. Simmer for 10mins or until the chicken has cooked through.

To serve, garnish with thinly sliced ginger and chopped cilantro leaves. Serve with a side of bread to enjoy!

Keema Matar

Popular in the Punjab area of Pakistan, this dish is a staple in every Punjabi-Pakistani's home. Minced meat is cooked off in delicious spices for a hearty and filling meal.

Makes: 4-6 servings

Prep: 10 mins

Cook: 10 mins

Ingredients:

- ½ cup oil
- 1 lb. mutton mince, washed and drained
- 1 cup shelled peas
- 8-10 cloves
- 1 inch piece cinnamon
- 8-10 peppercorns
- 2 large onions, chopped
- 10 cloves garlic, finely chopped
- 1 inch piece ginger, finely chopped
- 2 large tomatoes, chopped
- 2 tsp salt
- 1 ½ tsp red chili powder
- 1 ½ tsp garam masala powder
- 1 tsp turmeric powder
- Garnish
- ¼ cup fresh cilantro, chopped
- ½ inch ginger, thinly sliced

Directions:

Wash the mince in a strainer. Press to drain out the water well.

Heat oil in a pressure cooker. Add in the cloves, cinnamon and peppercorns. Cook for 1 minute.

Add in the chopped onions, ginger, and garlic. Fry till onions turn a rich brown in color.

Add in the tomatoes, spices and the mince mutton. Cook until oil starts rising to the top.

Add in the peas and mix well. Add in ¾ cups water and close the pressure cooker. Cook for 3 whistle rounds.

To serve, remove in a serving dish and garnish with fresh cilantro, chopped ginger and lemon wedges! Enjoy with bread or rice!

Achar Chicken

Translating to Pickled Chicken, strong **Ingredients** are used to give this dish its trademark flavor. Serve with tandoori roti!

Makes: 12 servings

Prep: 10 mins

Cook: 20 mins

Ingredients:

- 2 lbs. chicken
- 6 tbsp. cooking oil
- 2 onions, finely chopped
- 2 tsp cumin
- 4 pieces green chili, chopped
- 2 tbsp. ginger paste
- 2 tbsp. garlic paste
- 1 1/2 cups tomato puree
- Salt as per taste
- 2 tsp turmeric
- 2 tbsp. red chili powder
- 2 tsp crushed red chili
- 2 tsp cilantro powder
- 2 tsp cumin powder
- 1 tsp fennel
- 1 tsp mustard seeds
- 1 tsp fenugreek seeds
- 1 tsp nigella seeds
- 4 tbsp. pickle, chopped
- One cup hot water

Directions:

In a large pan, heat the oil. Add in the onion, cumin and green chili. Cook for 2 mins.

Add in the pastes, and chicken and cook for 2-3 minutes before adding the remaining ingredients.

Cook for an additional minute before adding half a cup of hot water. Allow to simmer for 8-10 minutes on low

Garnish with sliced ginger and fresh cilantro leaves. Serve.

Black Pepper Beef

If you like pepper, this recipe is going to be a new favorite. Succulent pieces of beef are cooked off in an aromatic and flavorsome stew. Perfect with some Rumali or Tandoori Roti.

Makes: 8 servings

Prep: 10 mins

Cook: 15 mins

Ingredients:

- 2 lb. beef, cut into bite sized pieces
- 2 large onions, finely sliced
- 4-5 green chilies, slit in half
- 2 tbsp. garlic paste
- 1 tbsp. ginger paste
- ¼ tsp turmeric
- 1 tbsp. crushed black pepper
- Salt to taste
- 1 cup water
- 2 tbsp. cilantro leaves

Directions:

Heat oil in a pressure cooker, then add in the sliced onions and green chilies. Cook till onion is translucent.

Add in the beef, ginger and garlic paste, and turmeric. Cook for 2 minutes.

Then add in the crushed black pepper, salt to taste and 1 cup water. Cover and cook for one whistle. Once it whistles, lower the heat and allow to cook for 10-15 minutes until has pressure has been released.

Once released, open the lid and continue simmering until thickened.

Add in the cilantro leaves and additional pepper if desired.

Chicken Jalfrezi

A traditional spicy Pakistani curry with garlic, chili and ginger.

Makes: 6 servings

Prep: 10 mins

Cook: 30 mins

Ingredients:

- 2 Tbsp. of vegetable oil
- 1 onion, grated
- 2 cloves of garlic, chopped
- 1 ½ lbs. chicken thighs, boneless, skinless and cut in 1/2
- 3 tsp. of powdered turmeric
- 1 tsp. of powdered chili
- 1 ½ tsp. of salt
- 1 14.5 ounce can of tomatoes, peeled and chopped
- 2 Tbsp. of ghee
- 3 tsp. of ground cumin
- 3 tsp. of powdered coriander
- 2 Tbsp. of ginger root, grated
- ½ cup cilantro, chopped

Directions:

In a skillet set over medium to high, add the vegetable oil. Add the grated onion and chopped garlic. Cook for 2 to 3 minutes.

Add in the chicken.

Season with the powdered turmeric, powdered chili and dash of salt. Stir well to mix. Cook for 5 to 10 minutes or until the chicken is cooked through.

Add in the can of tomatoes along with the juice from the can. Cover and cook for 20 minutes over low heat. Remove the lid and continue to cook for 10 minutes.

Add in the ghee, ground cumin, grated ginger root, powdered coriander and chopped cilantro. Stir well until evenly blended. Cook for 5 to 8 minutes.

Remove and serve immediately.

Pakistani Methi Chicken

This is a restaurant quality Pakistani dish that is not only incredibly easy to make, but with it being made with fresh herbs, one of the tastiest.

Makes: 4 servings

Prep: 10 mins

Cook: 25 mins

Ingredients:

- 1 pound of chicken bones, cut into pieces
- 2 cups of fenugreek, chopped
- ¾ cup of yogurt, whisked until smooth
- 3 tomatoes, chopped
- 2 onions, chopped
- 10 cloves of garlic, chopped
- 1, 2 inch piece of ginger, grated
- 3 to 4 green chilies, chopped
- 1 ½ tsp. of powdered red chili
- 1 ½ tsp. of powdered coriander
- ½ tsp. of powdered turmeric
- 1 tsp. of powdered garam masala
- 1 tsp. of cumin seed
- 2 tsp. of lemon juice, 1 tsp. of white sugar
- 5 Tbsp. of vegetable oil
- Dash of salt
- Warm water, as needed
- 4 pods of green cardamom
- 8 to 10 whole peppercorns
- ½ tsp. of mace, crushed
- 4 cloves, whole

Directions:

In a saucepan set over medium to high heat, add in the vegetable oil. Add in the cumin seeds and cook for 30 seconds or until they begin to crackle.

Add in the onions. Increase the heat to high and cook for 1 minute.

Add in the pods of green cardamom, whole peppercorns, crushed mace and whole cloves. Stir well to mix. Cook for 5 minutes or until the onions are gold.

Add in the chicken bones, chopped tomatoes, chopped garlic and grated ginger. Stir well to mix. Cook for 2 minutes.

Lower the heat to low. Add in the whisked yogurt and stir well to incorporate.

Add in the powdered red chili, powdered turmeric, powdered coriander, powdered cumin and dash of salt. Add in the warm water. Stir well until evenly mixed. Cover and cook for 8 minutes or until the chicken is soft.

Add in the fenugreek, lemon juice, powdered garam masala and white sugar. Stir well to evenly incorporate. Cook for an additional 1 to 2 minutes.

Remove from heat and serve immediately.

Shaami Kebab

Crispy meat shells filled with a surprise center come together to form these kebabs.

Makes: 20 Kebabs

Prep: 20 mins

Cook: 15 mins

Ingredients:

Meat:

- 2 lb. beef
- 5 cups water
- 1 cup gram lentils, washed through
- ½ cumin powder
- 10 dried red chili pods
- ½ tsp cardamom powder
- 1 tsp black pepper
- 12 garlic cloves, crushed
- ½ tsp cinnamon
- 1 small piece ginger, finely chopped
- ½ tsp cilantro seeds
- 1 tbsp. yogurt
- 1 egg, beaten
- Salt to taste

Filling:

- ½ cup fresh cilantro
- 1 inch piece ginger
- ½ cup fresh mint
- 1 large onion

Directions:

In a large saucepan, combine all the meat ingredients except for the egg. Bring the mixture to a boil. Continue cooking once meat turns tender and is completely cooked through. Remove from heat and allow to cool.

As the meat cooks, prepare the filling. Place all ingredients into a chopper and process till finely chopped. Remove and set aside.

Add in the meat mixture and process until smooth.

Remove into a bowl and add in the beaten egg. Mix well until thoroughly combined.

To start making the kebabs, take about 2 tbsp. of the meat mixture and roll it into a ball. Flatten it lightly and using your finger, create a small indent in the center. Add about a tsp of the filling mixture and cover with the sides, creating a round shape. Flatten to create a thick disk.

Repeat with the rest of the mixture.

To fry the kebabs, heat about 2 tbsp. oil in a frying pan and place kebabs in. Fry on both sides about 2-3 minutes until crispy and golden.

Garnish with cilantro leaves and onion slices and serve.

Haleem

Usually made during large social gatherings, Haleem is a staple celebratory dish in Pakistan.

Makes: 8 servings

Prep: 3 hrs.

Cook: 30 mins

Ingredients:

Grains:

- 1 cup wheat grain
- ¼ cup barley
- ¼ cup golden gram lentil
- ¼ cup green lentils
- ¼ cup long grain rice (basmati is preferred)
- 1 cup Chana dal (split Bengal gram lentils)
- ¼ cup white lentils

Haleem:

- ½ to ¾ cup oil
- 2 ½ lbs. boneless beef (you may also use veal if preferred)
- 1 ½ large onions, thinly sliced
- 1 ½ cup beef stock
- 1 ½ tbsp. red chili powder
- Salt to taste
- 1 tbsp. garlic paste
- 1 tbsp. ginger paste
- 1 tbsp. coriander powder
- 1 ½ tsp turmeric powder

For steaming:

- 1 tsp garam masala powder
- ¼ tsp nutmeg powder
- ¼ tsp mace powder
- ½ tsp black cumin
- ½ tsp cardamom powder

Directions:

Soak all grains for 6-8 hours. This is best done overnight.

In a large pan, heat oil. Add onion and cook until golden brown.

Add in the meat, garlic paste, ginger paste, chili powder, turmeric, coriander powder, and stock. Salt to taste.

Cook until the meat is tender.

In a separate deep set pan, boil pre-soaked grains for 2-2 ½ hours or until tender.

Once boiled, roughly blend the grains in a food processor. Transfer the crushed grains back to the pan to cook further.

Repeat the blending process with the meat mixture before adding it to the grains.

Combine well and continue cooking on low, stirring constantly.

Cook until the Haleem resembles a very thick chili. Season to taste.

Finally, add in the steam ingredients and mix thoroughly. Cover the pan and allow to steam for a few minutes before serving.

To serve, place in a large serving dish with accompaniments of chopped ginger, chilies, and deep fried onions!

Note –

To make the deep fried onions, simply slice 2 large onions and deep fry until dark brown.

Moong Dal

This is a common and authentic Pakistani dish that is typically served on an everyday basis in Pakistan.

Makes: 4 servings

Prep: 35 mins

Cook: 35 mins

Ingredients:

- 2 cups of dried yellow split peas
- 1 cup of tomatoes, chopped
- 1 onion, thinly sliced
- 1 tsp. of powdered red chili
- ½ tsp. of powdered coriander
- ½ tsp. of powdered turmeric
- Dash of black pepper
- 3 cloves, whole
- 2 pods of cardamom
- 1 bay leaf
- 4 leaves of curry
- 1 tsp. of powdered garam masala
- 2 Tbsp. of lemon juice
- 2 cloves of garlic, thinly sliced
- ½ tsp. of garlic paste
- ½ tsp. of ground cumin
- 2 dried red chili peppers
- 2 Tbsp. of coriander leaves, chopped
- 2 green chilies, chopped
- Dash of salt
- 3 Tbsp. of ghee
- 1 Tbsp. of vegetable oil

Directions:

Wash the dried split peas under running water. Transfer into a bowl and cover with water. Allow to soak for 30 to 35 minutes.

In a saucepan set over medium to high heat, add in the drained split peas, powdered red chili, powdered coriander, powdered turmeric and garlic paste. Stir well to mix and allow to come to a boil. Cook for 10 to 12 minutes.

Add in the chopped tomatoes and chopped green chilies. Cook for 10 minutes or until soft.

Add in the bay leaves, fresh lemon juice, dash of salt and powdered garam masala. Stir well to mix.

In a saucepan set over medium to high heat, add in the vegetable oil, add in the sliced onion. Cook for 5 minutes or until gold.

In a separate skillet, add in the ghee. Add in the cumin seeds, whole cloves, dash of black pepper, pods of cardamom, chopped curry leaves, red chilies and garlic. Stir well to mix. Cook for 5 minutes.

Remove from heat and serve with a garnish of chopped coriander.

Aloo Tikki

This delicious potato crisps are a great way to start off any dinner or even as quick snacks for cold evenings!

Makes: 8 servings

Prep: 25 mins

Cook: 15 mins

Ingredients:

- 2 lb. potatoes
- 2 hardboiled eggs
- 4 green chilies
- ½ cup fresh cilantro, chopped
- 1 medium onion, finely chopped
- 1 tsp black pepper powder
- 1 tsp cumin powder
- Salt to taste
- 1 cup breadcrumbs
- 1 egg
- Oil

Directions:

Thoroughly rinse the potatoes and boil with skins on until soft. Remove from water and allow to cool slightly before removing skins.

Mash the potatoes and the hardboiled until smooth and free of lumps.

Add the chilies, cilantro, onion and spices. Season according to taste. Combine evenly

Once combined, allow to chill for 15-20 minutes before forming the patties.

Beat the egg in a bowl and place the breadcrumbs in another.

To form the patties, place about 2 tbsp. of the potato mixture into your palm and roll into a ball shape. Flatten to form a thick disk.

Dip into the egg and then coat with the breadcrumbs.

Do this with the rest of the potato mixture until all your patties have been formed.

Deep fry on low heat until golden brown. Drain on a paper towel.

Serve warm and enjoy!

Punjabi Samosa

Crispy, crunchy exterior holds a spiced potato filling that is sure to leave you wanting more!

Makes: 10 servings

Prep: 20 mins

Cook: 10 mins

Ingredients:

Samosa Dough –

- 2 ½ cup all-purpose flour
- 1 tsp ajwain (carom seed)
- 1 tsp salt
- 4 tbsp. ghee or oil
- Water

Filling –

- 2 tbsp. ghee or oil
- 1 tsp cumin
- 1 inch ginger, chopped
- 4-5 potatoes, boiled and mashed
- ½ tsp mango powder
- 1 tsp red chili powder
- 1 tsp cilantro powder
- 1 tsp garam masala

Pomegranate mixture -

- 1 tbsp cilantro powder
- 1 tsp dried pomegranate

Directions:

To make the dough, combine all the Ingredients together and just enough water to create a tough dough. Cover and set aside.

To make the filling, heat the ghee in a pan. Add in the rest of the Ingredients and cook until combined.

In a separate small pan, roast the 1 tbsp. of cilantro powder and 1 tsp of pomegranate seeds. Once roasted, crush into a rough paste.

Add this paste to the potato mixture and combine thoroughly.

To make the samosas, divide the dough into 10 pieces.

Roll each piece into a circle of 1/8 inch thickness and cut it into half, giving you 2 semi circles.

Place a bowl of water next to you and move onto the next step.

Hold one corner of the semi-circle and rolling the dough into a cone shape, overlap with the other corner, sticking them together with some water.

Fill the cone with the potato mixture, making sure to leave about ¼ - ½ inch of dough on top. Press the top of the cone together with some water to finish making the samosa.

Do this with the rest of the dough and potato mixture.

Heat oil on low. Make sure the oil is not too hot because we don't want the samosas to burn.

Fry the samosas on low for about 8-10 minutes until crisp and brown.

Serve with your favorite sauces or condiments and enjoy!

Bhuna Gosht

This is a delicious Pakistani dish made with mutton and cardamom.

Makes: 4 servings

Prep: 10 mins

Cook: 20 mins

Ingredients:

- 1 tomato, cut into slices
- 1 onion, chopped
- pounds of mutton, chopped
- Tbsp. of garlic and ginger paste
- ½ tsp. of tsp. of cumin seed
- Powdered red chili
- Dash of salt
- ¼ tsp. of powdered turmeric
- pods of black cardamom
- 5 pods of green cardamom
- 6 Tbsp. of butter, soft

Directions:

In a pot, add the mutton pieces. Season with a dash of salt and powdered turmeric. Cook over low heat and cook for 5 minutes.

Add in the soft butter into a separate skillet. Add the cumin seed and cook for 1 minute or until toasted. Add the onion and cook for 5 minutes or until soft.

Add in the tomato slices. Cook for 5 minutes or until soft.

Add in the ginger and garlic paste. Stir well to incorporate.

Add in the mutton pieces and powdered chili. Cook for an additional minute.

Grind the black and green cardamom pods until powdery in consistency. Add to the mutton. Stir well to mix. Cook for 30 seconds or until aromatic.

Remove and serve immediately.

Rice Pudding

This is a highly popular dessert served in Pakistan.

Makes: 6 servings

Prep: hr.

Cook: hr. 0 mins

Ingredients:

- ½ cup of white rice
- 2 quarts of whole milk
- ½ cups of white sugar
- 4 pods of cardamom
- 2 tsp. of rose water
- ¼ cup of almonds, chopped

Directions:

In a bowl, add the white rice and cover with water. Set aside to soak for hour.

Drain the rice and transfer into a saucepan set over low heat. Add the whole milk. Cook for 50 minutes or until the rice is soft.

Add in the white sugar and pods of cardamom. Continue to cook for an additional 20 minutes.

Remove from heat. Add the rose water and stir well until incorporated.

Serve immediately with the chopped almonds over the top.

Chapli Kebab

These deliciously moist kebabs with a kick of spices are a local favorite.

Makes: 20 kebabs

Prep: 20 mins

Cook: 0 mins

Ingredients:

- 2 lb. mince beef
- tsp red chili powder
- ½ tsp black pepper
- tsp Cilantro
- tsp cumin powder
- 4 green chilies, finely chopped
- onion, finely sliced
- 4 tomatoes, finely chopped
- bunch fresh mint leaves, finely chopped
- bunch fresh Cilantro, finely chopped
- egg
- Salt to taste
- Oil to fry.

Directions:

Mix all the kebab ingredients in a food process and process until evenly mixed but not too fine.

Move the mixture to a bowl and chill for 5 minutes.

To form the kebabs, take about ½ tbsp. of the meat mixture and roll into a smooth ball. Flatten between your palms. Repeat with the rest of the mixture to make the remaining kebabs.

Heat a little oil in a frying pan – about 2-3 tbsp. Fry the kebabs, turning to ensure both sides are perfectly cooked until the kebabs turn brown and the meat is cooked through.

Garnish with onions and green chilies and serve.

Malai Chicken Tikka

Malai Chicken literally translates to Cream Chicken. The addition of thick cream to the marinade results in a juicy, grilled chicken that is chock full of flavor.

Makes: 6 servings

Prep: 6 hrs.

Cook: 0 mins

Ingredients:

- 2 lb. chicken, cut into inch pieces
- lb. yogurt
- 2 tbsp. thick cream
- tbsp. ginger paste
- tbsp. garlic paste
- tbsp. lemon juice
- Salt to taste
- tbsp. cumin powder
- 6-8 green chilies, chopped finely
- 3 tbsp. cilantro leaves
- 2 tbsp. almond paste (optional)

Directions:

In a medium bowl, mix together all ingredients and allow the chicken to marinate for at least hour in the fridge up to 6 hours (the longer, the better).

This next part is optional but highly recommended for maximum flavor – in a small, heat safe ramekin, place a piece of coal and light it. Place the ramekin into the bowl with the chicken and cover for 20 minutes. This lends a smoky flavor to the chicken.

Once smoked, heat oil in a large frying pan. Thread the chicken pieces onto metal skewers and fry until cooked through.

Garnish with onions and serve!

Seekh Kebab with Mint Chutney

A local favorite, these kebabs are a popular street food. Served with mint chutney, the kebabs are juicy and flavorsome.

Makes: 6 servings

Prep: 2 hrs.

Cook: 25 mins

Ingredients:

Kebab

- 2 lb. minced beef
- 2 medium sized onion
- green chilies
- tsp crushed green papaya
- /2 cup fresh cilantro
- ½ tsp cardamom powder
- tsp ground red chili powder
- tsp black pepper
- tsp garam masala
- 4 tbsp. chickpea flour
- egg

Chutney

- cup fresh mint leaves
- cup cilantro leaves
- ½ inch ginger
- green chili
- ½ tsp lemon juice
- ½ tsp cumin powder
- Pinch of salt

Directions:

Kebab

In a food processor, combine all the ingredients and process until mixed through.

Remove from mixer and knead thoroughly. This is important to allow the papaya paste to tenderize the meat.

Allow to develop for 2 hours in the fridge.

Once chilled, remove and knead once again.

Preheat oven to 450 F.

You can now begin forming the kebabs. Grab a metal skewer and roll the kebabs around the skewers.

Place the skewers on a grill rack and bake for 20-25 minutes rotating every now and then.

Remove from oven and serve warm fresh Cilantro chutney!

Chutney

To make the chutney, combine all the ingredients into a blender and mix together until smooth.

Serve in a small bowl with kebabs.

Chicken Cutlets

Fried Chicken gets a Pakistani makeover with these fun chicken cutlets that even picky eaters will find hard to put down!

Makes: 6 servings

Prep: 5 mins

Cook: 0 mins

Ingredients:

- whole chicken (3 lb.)
- clove garlic, crushed.
- hardboiled eggs
- 2 cups breadcrumbs
- medium onion, finely chopped
- 4 green chilies, finely chopped
- ½ cup fresh cilantro leaves
- tsp. black pepper
- Salt to taste
- 2 tbsp. soy sauce
- Oil for frying

Directions:

Wash the chicken thoroughly and boil it with the crushed garlic and a little bit of salt.

Once cooked, remove from water and allow to cool before separating meat from bones.

Put the chicken meat, boiled eggs, and breadcrumbs into a chopper and process until it turns into a smooth dry paste.

Add in the chopped greens chilies, onion, cilantro, black pepper, and soy sauce and combine thoroughly. Season with salt to taste.

Divide the mixture into small spheres and flatten slightly to form a thick disk.

Heat enough oil in a pan to shallow fry the cutlets and cook on both sides on low heat for 2-3 minutes until golden brown.

Serve warm and enjoy!

Nihari

Slow cooked meat in a delicious spiced stew is what makes Nihari one of the most popular dishes all over Pakistan. Enjoy with warm Tandoori Roti!

Makes: 4 servings

Prep: 0 mins

Cook: 40 mins

Ingredients:

- lb. lamb shank, cut into 2 inch pieces
- 2 ½ tbsp. Nihari Masala (homemade or store bought)
- 2 tbsp. pure ghee
- 2 medium onions, sliced and deep-fried till golden brown
- ½ inch ginger, cut into thin strips
- 2 tbsp. whole-wheat flour
- Salt to taste
- tbsp. lemon juice
- 2 tbsp. chopped fresh cilantro leaves
- Water
- Nihari Masala (optional, you can use store bought as well) -
- 2 tbsp. cumin seeds
- 2 tbsp. fennel seeds
- tbsp. cloves
- 3 green cardamoms
- black cardamoms
- 2-5 black peppercorns
- 2-3 tbsp. poppy seeds
- 6-8 whole dried red chilies
- bay leaves

- blade of mace

- tbsp. dried ginger powder

- 2-3 cinnamon sticks

- tbsp. nutmeg powder

- 2-3 tbsp. split chickpea powder

Directions:

Heat the ghee in pressure cooker. Add in the lamb and nihari masala and sauté for two mins.

Add 4 cups of water and cook under pressure till the pressure is released eight times (eight whistles). This may take about half an hour.

Remove lid when pressure has completely reduced and transfer the contents to a pan/wok. Bring the mixture to boil, stir in the fried onions and /2 the ginger and simmer for two minutes.

In a small bowl, mix the whole-wheat flour with six tbsp. of water and mix well till smooth.

Add to the lamb mixture and continue to simmer till the gravy thickens.

Add salt and stir in the lemon juice.

To serve, garnish with the ginger and chopped cilantro leaves!

Nihari Masala

To make the nihari masala, roast all the Ingredients in a frying pan till fragrant. Remove from heat and set aside to cool.

Once cooled, blitz to a fine powder and store in an airtight container for use.

Green Murgh Masala

This delicious chicken recipe gets its signature green hue from the fresh mint and cilantro leaves added in!

Makes: 8 servings

Prep: 0 mins

Cook: 20 mins

Ingredients:

- 2 lb. skinless chicken breasts, cut into bite sized pieces
- 2 medium sized onions, finely chopped
- 2 -inch piece ginger, roughly chopped
- 8-0 cloves garlic, roughly chopped
- ½ cup fresh cilantro leaves, chopped
- tbsp. fresh mint leaves, chopped
- 6-8 green chilies
- ½ cup yogurt
- Salt to taste
- 3 tbsp. oil
- 4 green cardamoms
- inch piece cinnamon
- tbsp. coriander powder
- tbsp. cumin powder
- ½ cup cream
- tsp garam masala powder

Directions:

Slit two green chilies and set aside.

Combine the rest of the green chilies, ginger, garlic, cilantro, and mint leaves and grind together.

In a large bowl, combine this mixture with yogurt and add salt to taste.

Add in the chicken pieces and allow to marinade for an hour in the fridge.

Heat oil in a large pan; add the cardamom, cinnamon and the slit green chilies. Cook for a minute and then add in the onions. Cook until translucent.

Add in the coriander and cumin powders and cook for minute.

Add in the chicken along with the excess marinate. Cook on medium heat for 2 minutes, then cover and cook for 0-5 minutes until chicken has cooked through. Add in water if required.

Once cooked, adjust seasoning, stir in fresh cream and sprinkle on the garam masala. Mix thoroughly.

Simmer for 2 minutes and serve!

Besan Ladoo

A classic Pakistani ladoo recipe with chickpea flour.

Makes: 0 servings

Prep: 2 hrs. 0 mins

Cook: 0 mins

Ingredients:

- ¾ cup of ghee
- 2 cups of chickpea flour
- ½ cup of sweet coconut, shredded
- 3 Tbsp. of ground almonds
- ½ cup of castor sugar
- ½ tsp. of powdered cardamom

Directions:

In a wok set over low heat, add in the ghee. Add in the chickpea flour. Cook for 0 minutes or until toasted.

Remove and allow to cool for 5 minutes.

In a coffee grinder or food processor, add in the shredded coconut. Grind until fine in consistency.

Add in the ground almonds, castor sugar, ground coconuts and powdered cardamom into the wok. Stir well to mix.

Shape the mix into balls that are inch in diameter. Place onto a baking sheet.

Set aside to rest for 2 to 3 hours before serving.

Rumali Roti

Rumali, translating to handkerchief perfectly describes these super thin, see through rotis! They are fun to eat and make!

Makes: 2 servings

Prep: 25 mins

Cook: 0 mins

Ingredients:

Dough

- cups all-purpose flour
- 2 tsp salt
- 4 tsp oil
- ½ cup warm water, add as needed
- ½ cup extra flour to dust

Salt Water

- 2 cups water
- 2 tsp salt

Directions:

In a bowl, mix the salt, flour & 2 tsp of oil.

Add in the milk in increments, kneading in between. Knead for at least 5 minutes.

Once the dough has come together, roll into a large ball and coat with remaining 2 tsp of oil.

Cover with a cloth & leave to rest for 20 minutes. Knead again for 5 minutes.

To make the roti, divide the dough into 2 balls. Start rolling out the dough, dusting with flour if needed to prevent sticking. Roll out as thin as possible.

Heat a pan & spray with cooking spray.

Carefully roll the roti over your rolling pin and unroll over the pan. Cook on both sides for2 minutes or until lightly brown on both sides.

Serve warm with main dish of your choice!

Gulab Jamun

This is a highly popular and traditional Pakistani dessert.

Makes: 0 servings

Prep: 0 mins

Cook: 20 mins

Ingredients:

For Gulab:

- cup of powdered milk
- 2 tbsp. of all-purpose flour
- tsp. of semolina
- egg, beaten
- tsp. of baker's style baking powder

Ingredients for the sheera:

- 2 cups of water
- 2 cups of white sugar
- ¼ tsp. of powdered green cardamom

Directions:

Prepare the gulab. In a bowl, add in all of the Ingredients for the gulab. Stir well until smooth in consistency.

Shape the mix into 5 to 20 balls. Set onto a plate.

In a frying pan, add 2 to 3 tablespoons of vegetable oil. Add in the balls. Fry for 5 minutes or until gold.

Prepare the sheera. In a separate saucepan, add in the water and white sugar. Whisk until mixed. Allow to come to a boil. Cook for 5 to 8 minutes or until syrupy in consistency. Add in the powdered green cardamom. Remove and set aside to cool.

Pour the sheera over the fried gulab. Toss until coated thoroughly.

Set aside to rest for 35 to 40 minutes before serving.

Gosht Do Piyaza

This dish uses onions in two different ways lending it the name do piyaza, which translates to 2 onions. It is rich, jam packed with flavor and goes well with Tandoori roti!

Makes: 6 servings

Prep: 0 mins

Cook: 50 mins

Ingredients:

- 2 lb. boneless lamb, cut into bite sized pieces
- large onions
- ½ cup oil
- inch cinnamon
- 0 green cardamoms
- 0 cloves
- 2 tsp garlic paste
- tbsp. coriander powder
- 2 tsp cumin powder
- 2 tsp ginger paste
- tbsp. yogurt, whisked
- ½ tsp red chili powder
- Salt to taste
- ½ tsp garam masala powder

Directions:

Cut three onions in half vertically, and then slice them finely into half rings. Chop the remaining onion finely.

Heat the oil in a large pan; add the finely sliced onions and cook till golden. Remove using a slotted spoon onto a paper towel lined plate.

Add the cinnamon, cardamoms and cloves to the oil remaining in the pan and sauté over medium heat till they begin to sizzle. Add the lamb cubes, a few at a time, and sauté till brown. Remove the lamb with a slotted spoon and place in a bowl.

Add the chopped onion to the same pan and sauté till golden. Add the garlic and ginger pastes and sauté over medium heat till the oil separates. Add the coriander powder and cumin powder and continue to sauté for half a minute.

Add the yogurt, one tablespoon at a time, and sauté till well combined.

Add the lamb cubes, ½ cup of water, chili powder and salt. Mix well and bring the mixture to a boil. Cover the pan, lower heat and cook for about 45 minutes until the lamb is tender.

Add the fried onions & garam masala powder and mix well. Continue to cook, uncovered, for another two or three minutes, stirring gently. Serve hot!

Sindhi Biryani

The most popular biryani in Pakistan is the Sindhi biryani. Moist pieces of chicken rest on delicious spiced rice. The aroma of this dish is to die for!

Makes: 4 servings

Prep: 4 hrs.

Cook: 20 mins

Ingredients:

Marinade

- 2 lb. mutton, cut into bite sized pieces
- cup yogurt
- ½ tbsp. ginger paste
- ½ tbsp. garlic paste
- Salt to taste

Biryani -

- tbsp. red chili powder
- 2 tbsp. coriander powder
- ½ cups Basmati rice
- tbsp. allspice
- ½ cup dried apricots (soak in hot water)
- green chilies
- bay leaf
- medium onions, finely sliced
- lb. potatoes, peeled and diced into inch pieces
- 4 tomatoes
- cup oil

Directions:

In a bowl, combine the meat, yogurt, salt, ginger paste and garlic paste. Marinate for about 4 hours to overnight in a refrigerator.

In a pan, heat the oil. Add in the onions and cook until golden brown. Remove half the onions using a slotted spoon and place on a paper towel laid plate.

Add in the meat along with the marinade mixture. Sprinkle on the spices and cook until the mixture has dried out and the meat is tender. Add in the potatoes, tomatoes, apricots and green chilies. Cook on high for 5 minutes, stirring constantly. Remove from heat and keep aside.

In a large, deep pan, bring 2 cups of water to a boil. Add in the bay leaf. Season to taste. Once the water starts boiling, add in the rice. Parboil, and strain.

Start layering the rice with the meat mixture starting and ending with the rice. Cook for 0-5 minutes more or until rice has cooked through.

Garnish with mint leaves and serve warm!

Butter Chicken

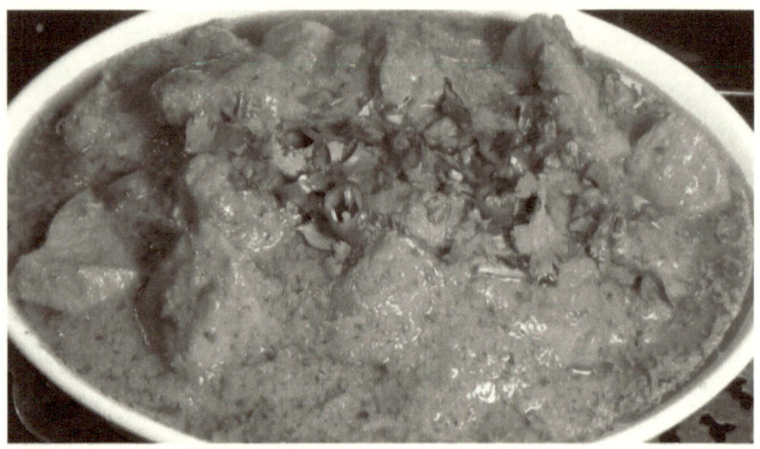

If you want to serve a traditional Pakistani dish to your friends and family, then this is one dish you can't go wrong with.

Makes: 4 servings

Prep: 0 mins

Cook: 20 mins

Ingredients:

- ¼ pint of yogurt
- 2 ounces of ground almonds
- ½ tsp. of powdered chili
- ¼ tsp. of crushed bay leaves
- ¼ tsp. of ground cloves
- ¼ tsp. of ground cinnamon
- tsp. of garam masala
- pods of green cardamom
- tsp. of ginger pulp
- tsp. of garlic pulp
- , 4 ounce can of tomatoes, chopped
- Dash of salt
- 2 pounds of chicken, skinless and cut into small cubes
- 3 ounces of butter
- Tbsp. of corn oil
- 2 onions, thinly sliced
- 2 Tbsp. of coriander, chopped
- 4 Tbsp. of heavy whipping cream

Directions:

In a bowl, add in the yogurt, ground almonds, crushed bay leaves, powdered chili, ground cloves, powdered cinnamon, garam masala, pods of green cardamom, ginger pulp, and garlic pulp. Stir well until evenly mixed.

Add in the chicken and toss well to coat. Set aside for later use.

In a skillet set over medium to high heat, add in the butter and corn oil. Add in the thinly sliced onions. Cook for 5 minutes or until soft.

Add in the chicken mix. Cook for 0 minutes or until the chicken is cooked.

Add in half of the coriander and stir well to mix.

Add in the heavy whipping cream and stir gently to incorporate. Allow to come to a boil.

Remove from heat and garnish with the chopped coriander over the top.

Sheer Khurma

Traditionally cooked on Eid, Sheer Khurma is a widely known milk dessert that is quick, easy and very satisfying!

Makes: 6 servings

Prep: 0 mins

Cook: 20 mins

Ingredients:

- ½ cups + 2 tbsp. milk,
- /3 cups dry vermicelli
- 8-0 almonds
- 8-0 pistachios
- 2-3 strands of saffron
- 2 tbsp. ghee
- ¼ tsp cardamom powder
- Pinch of nutmeg powder
- 2 tbsp. sunflower seeds
- ½ cup sugar

Directions:

Blanch the almonds & pistachios in boiling water. Drain, peel and cut into slivers.

In a bowl put the saffron in 2 tbsp. of warm milk.

In a large pan, heat the ghee. Add in the vermicelli and stir for about 3-4 minutes or until light golden.

Add in 7 ½ cups of milk and bring to a boil. Once it boils, reduce & simmer till the milk thickens and changes color slightly.

Add in the cardamom, nutmeg, saffron mixture, sunflower seeds, almonds, pistachios and sugar. Continue to cook for an extra 0 mins and then remove from heat.

Serve warm and enjoy!

Shahi Tukra

A spiced milk soaked bread pudding with garnish nuts, Shahi Tukra is delicious and warm ending to any meal.

Makes: 6 servings

Prep: 0 mins

Cook: 5 mins

Ingredients:

- slices white bread cut in half
- 4 cups milk
- cup sugar
- cardamom pods
- cup milk powder
- Pinch of saffron
- ½ cup ghee or butter
- 0 almonds
- 0 pistachios

Directions:

Black the nuts in water and chop roughly once cooled. Set aside.

Heat the ghee or butter in a frying pan. Fry off the bread slices until golden brown. Remove and leave on paper towel.

Wipe off the excess grease from the pan and add in the milk. Bring to a boil. Once the milk starts boiling, add in the cardamom, sugar, and milk powder. Cook on low for an additional 5 minutes.

Once the milk starts to thicken, add in the saffron. Remove from heat and allow to cool slightly.

To assemble, layer 4 triangles in tray and pour in half the milk mixture. Allow the bread to absorb the milk.

Top with the remaining bread slices and pour in the rest of the milk. Let the dish cool completely.

Sprinkle with the chopped nuts and serve!

Carrot Halwa

This carrot halwa gives you all new reasons to load up on carrots on your next grocery run!

Makes: 8 servings

Prep: 0 mins

Cook: 25 mins

Ingredients:

Halwa

- cups carrot, grated
- 4 cups milk
- tbsp. ghee or unsalted butter
- ½ cup sugar
- tsp cardamom powder
- ¼ cup walnut, roughly chopped
- almonds, blanched and slivered

Garnish

- Slivered almonds
- Slivered cashews

Directions:

In a medium saucepan, heat ½ a tsp of ghee or butter and toast the slivered almonds. Once they turn brown, remove and set aside.

Wipe off the excess butter and add in the milk. Bring to a boil and allow to cook till the milk has reduced in half to about 2 cups. Stir constantly so as not to burn the milk at the bottom.

In a separate frying pan, heat the rest of the ghee or butter and add in the carrots. Fry for about 7-8 minutes until the carrots become tender and darken in color.

Add in the milk and continue cooking until the mixture is no longer wet and liquid. About 8-0 minutes.

Add in the sugar, walnuts and cardamom. Cook for an additional 3 minutes, stirring constantly.

Serve warm garnished with almonds and cashews!

Ras Malai

Milk doughnuts in a sweet milk syrup, ras malai is a very popular street dessert throughout Pakistan.

Makes: 8 servings

Prep: hr. 5 mins

Cook: 5 mins

Ingredients:

For the Rasmalai:

- cups milk
- 4 tbsp. lemon juice
- tsp. cornstarch
- 4 cups water, divided
- cup sugar
- 2 tbsp. all-purpose flour

Milk Syrup

- 4 cups milk
- ½ cup sugar
- 5-6 pistachios, blanched and cut into slivers.

Directions:

First make the curdled cheese needed to make the dough. In a saucepan, take the 4 cups of milk to a boil. Once boiling, remove from heat and add in ½ cup of water to lower the temperature of the milk.

Allow to cool for 5-0 minutes and then add in the lemon juice to curdle.

Let curdle for 5 minutes and then using a strainer, collect the curdled cheese while ridding it of liquid. Allow it to strain for 0-5 minutes and then using your hands, lightly squeeze the cheese to remove excess liquid.

In a bowl, add in the cheese and cornstarch and knead for 0 minutes until completely smooth.

Divide into 8 equal portions and roll into balls. Set aside.

In a large pan, combine 3 ½ cups of water and sugar and bring to a boil. Add the flour and stir.

Carefully place the rasmalai dough balls into this liquid and allow to cook for 0 minutes on high. After 0 minutes, add in half a cup of water and boil for 3 more minutes. Remove from heat and let the balls rest in the liquid.

To make the milk syrup, boil the milk in a thick saucepan until thickened slightly.

Add in the sugar and continue boiling until the sugar has melted through. Remove from heat and allow to cool. Once cooled, refrigerate for an hour.

Lightly squeeze the cooked rasmalai balls and place into the milk mixture. Refrigerate for another hour to infuse.

Serve chilled, garnished with pistachios!

Conclusion

Well, there you go! 30 delicious recipes all the way from Pakistan for you to try! Make sure to try out all these flavorful and delicious recipes, and don't forget to share them with your friends and family too!

About the Author

Allie Allen developed her passion for the culinary arts at the tender age of five when she would help her mother cook for their large family of 8. Even back then, her family knew this would be more than a hobby for the young Allie and when she graduated from high school, she applied to cooking school in London. It had always been a dream of the young chef to study with some of Europe's best and she made it happen by attending the Chef Academy of London.

After graduation, Allie decided to bring her skills back to North America and open up her own restaurant. After 10 successful years as head chef and owner, she decided to sell her business and pursue other career avenues. This monumental decision led Allie to her true calling, teaching. She also started to write e-books for her students to study at home for practice. She is now the proud author of several e-books and gives private and semi-private cooking lessons to a range of students at all levels of experience.

Stay tuned for more from this dynamic chef and teacher when she releases more informative e-books on cooking and baking in the near future. Her work is infused with stores and anecdotes you will love!

Author's Afterthoughts

I can't tell you how grateful I am that you decided to read my book. My most heartfelt thanks that you took time out of your life to choose my work and I hope you find benefit within these pages.

There are so many books available today that offer similar content so that makes it even more humbling that you decided to buying mine.

Tell me what you thought! I am eager to hear your opinion and ideas on what you read as are others who are looking for a good book to buy. Leave a review on Amazon.com so others can benefit from your wisdom!

With much thanks,

Allie Allen